One Foot In

Jeff Pew

NeoPoiesisPress.com

NeoPoiesis Press, LLC

2775 Harbor Ave SW, Suite D, Seattle, WA
For more info: Info@NeoPoiesisPress.com
NeoPoiesisPress.com

Jeff Pew – One Foot In
ISBN 978-0-9975021-4-5 (paperback: alk. paper)

    1. Poetry. I. Pew, Jeff. II. One Foot In.

Library of Congress Control Number: 2016915427

First Edition

Design, art direction and typography: Milo Duffin and Stephen Roxborough
Back cover photography: Kalum Ko

Printed in the United States of America

for Alison and the boys

Contents

IV: Before the First Poem

V: One Dies One's Life

I: A Good Window

merely lets in the light
like the 'oo' in booze.

My Confusion with Everything

Remember the good old days
when we could say something stupid
in the bar? Our kids, one-eyed, silly and toothless.
The breezy calm of lawn darts
slingshots and falling from trees.
Sprawled in the sun
we were baby-oil burnt
crackled-pork skin.

Who doesn't feel a little cheated?
AKA the wool pulled over our eyes.
Gone is the simple retribution of a slug in the head.
The clunky charm of the Imperial system.
The V8 sedation of a Sunday drive.
Who doesn't long to toss a bucket
of feces out the window?
Blame bad weather on witchcraft.

Thank God for the infidels.

This prickly protocol of the new normal:
Can we masturbate without going blind?
Swallow our chewing gum?
What about these leeches stuck to our chest?

Wasn't it enough, when they took
the cocaine out of Cola?
Forced us to strap our kids
into the back seat of a car.
Forbid them to stick their heads
out the window, feel the sting of wind
the thrill of a bug exploding in their eye.

Before it's over, some heretic
will come screaming:

the world is as round as an orange
the navel of an infinite universe.
Our gravity, so immense
stars will yearn to comfort us.

Twinkle as if everything is all right.

Everyone in My Way

A car meanders along an alpine road.
A negligee of dust lingers in the air. Ahead
a deer licks salt leeched from a clay bank.
A fly settles near its tail.
Nothing in a hurry.
Even an eagle, distracted by soaring, ignores
frolicking rodents below.

I honk. Flash my lights.
Scream obscenities out the window.
I rush to relax—roadrage to the river
study how a logjam swallows everything
too slow to turn. Who can't see how sluggish
we've become? Even the chestnut vendor
is calling it a day. Somewhere, a kid presses
every button in an elevator. Remember
when a glacier meant business?
We stutter at the amber light
terrified
of all the ways
we crash into each other.

There's Been a Terrible Mistake

Don't get me wrong.
I appreciate the applause
and everything you've done:
the mini-golf coupons, the masseuse
you sent to my room last night
those kind letters to my mother
apologizing for when I stole her cigarettes.
This Anne Murray paperweight
will make a perfect gift for my son.

But you got the wrong guy.
I pilfer from tsunami relief.
As a kid, I avoided milk.
I laugh when a robin crashes into a window.
I can't fix our toilet when it breaks.
Did I mention, this is a rental tuxedo?

Check under your seats. I have nothing to offer.
Look beside you. Your date is a stranger.
The building we're in has escaped.
My feet are too big for these shoes.
If I thought they deserved it, they'd ache.

But I promise to behave.
I will tip the maid.
Throw small fish back.
Pass out before getting too drunk.

Don't feel bad on my account.
Stick around. Let's have a drink.
Eat some cheese. Thank our lucky stars
we're not who we think we are.

She Keeps Coming Back

with her tight tidy hair,
her drab clothes
that lower the hem on summer.

I'm shirtless
paintbrush in one hand
beer in the other
and it's barely noon.

Still, I'm not beyond saving.

She pulls magazines from her purse
highlights articles about family values:
how splendid the earth will be
once all wickedness is cleansed.
"You'll like this one," she says.
A flock. A shepherd. An anointed one.
The overture of rewards.
A crew-cut boy in a white T-shirt
frolics with a tiger. A cartoon
waterfall licks his heels.

Satisfied, she smiles and leaves
one step closer to heaven.

I close the gate
rest dripping paint cans
on scattered magazines
a twitch of voices down the road.
I crack another beer.

Wait patiently
for paint to dry.

You Two Don't Fool Me

In the hotel elevator, a tourist
glances at our coffee cups and says
"You two don't fool me.
Come, let me buy you a drink."

I forget about the bucket of melted ice.
The concrete splat of tequila-soaked limes
tossed from our 19th floor balcony.
We stagger to an English Bay terrace.
A seagull mistakes a reflection
for clouds resting on our plates.
I wonder about my father-in-law
snoozing on the couch
chin on chest
the television muttering
about stardust and willow trees.

We toast the sun slipping behind a freighter
the piano player crooning about Jesus blowing up
balloons
our glasses smashing before they reach our lips.

You empty your pockets to a homeless woman
her hair slicked by rain.

We argue about which way is home
and whether we should sweep
leaves from the sidewalk.
We collapse on the dance floor
sleep on a tiny patch of grass in Barclay Park.
We search for a familiar star
a porch light, a sober neon sign.
I will throw up soon.

We look for the sea.
Anything that isn't solid.
Eventually, everything finds its way home.

River Lore

I wander through rivers
stumble over rocks
tiptoe between the certainty
of logjams and the grizzly bear
hidden behind the bush.
I fling a thin line into the current
a tiny hook disguised as a fly, moth, beetle
the succulent deception
of its blue-green belly.

I've got better things to do
than drag these fish to my knees
cradle them in my palm
twist hooks from pierced lips.

Yet, who can trust the tyranny
of evolution?

Before I return fish to water
I cast a stern stare.
I say, this is a scrap of foam.
This, a dry feather, rejected
by a peacock. Let the hook's glint
be your beacon. Let it remind you
of the cruelty of pointy things.

I'm teaching you a lesson:
how to become a better fish.

Until Our Cheeks Hurt

When she asked him to smile for their wedding photo, my grandfather refused. He claimed, despite being the happiest man in the world, he could never hold a smile that long. It was their first argument.

Moments before the plane arrived, Mr. Roarke gathered his staff and ordered them to smile. Upon docking, guests looked baffled, the glare of insincerity flashing in their faces. The only thing they could do: shield their eyes. Pretend to squint from the sun.

Over time, nothing was funny. She stood stiffly, clenched her nightgown in one hand, swatted a fly with the other. A cracked pain hidden in her face. As a little girl, her mother said, "*Try not to smile. You'll get wrinkles.*"

At a red light, on a summer day, in the back seat of a '73 Buick convertible, a pile of giggling girls sang *Crocodile Rock* to a woman at the crosswalk. The nervous boy in the front seat lip-synched, tried to smile along.

They posed between two willows. Branches, wisps of hair in her face. Barely visible, my grandfather's hand behind her head, holding back a strand of leaves. His austere gaze. A smile beneath his skin.

In November 1966, Brian Wilson encountered serious problems with *Smile*, exhibiting early signs of depression and paranoia. While recording the Fire section of the *Elements Suite* he became concerned the music was responsible for starting a rash of fires in the studio's neighbourhood.

An air-raid siren pierced the sky. In the bus station photo booth, he held a smile, and waited for a flash.

Lou Jacobs, the originator of the red rubber ball nose,
painted the same face every morning in his trailer.
He thought of the many ways a smile can go wrong.

We stare into the camera and force a cheesy grin.
We'll show them: these are happy times. No bedtimes.
No swift slaps to the back of the head. No sepia-stained
memories. Everything is perfect. A-Okay.

We'll smile until our cheeks hurt.

In the Bottom of a Drawer, a Microcassette

Here's the stop button. Say hello.
What would you like to talk about?
I have a burnt tongue.
We want you to become a nuclear scientist.

I think I have your keys.
I think I have some money for you.
Too bad things didn't work out.
We have to justify why we are alive.

You have to decide what it is you want to say.
If you are there, pick up the phone.
I stepped on a robin I knocked from the air.

We're all practising here.

A Trail of Crumbs

I wander into traffic,
notice a sign suggesting I turn left.
My dad, up to his old tricks again.
One day, it's *Watch for Falling Rock*,
the next, a weathervane pointing east.
I stalk a trail of bread crumbs
he scattered before dying.
On sad days, I wonder
if they weren't left for crows, robins
or waxwings seeking sobriety.
At the drive-thru a muffled voice
offers homespun advice
about the value of hard work
and asks for forgiveness.
In the crackled static, the message
is distorted. Something about
sugar and cream.
On the overpass, a battered pickup
slows and offers me a ride.
I snicker at how predictable life is:
the straw clenched between his teeth,
the annoying way our sun
always sets.

Bargain of the Year

i.
Popular Science, 1956.
Times like these, everybody
must pull their own weight.
Nothing to lose.
The most important day
in your life. The art talent
you never dreamed of. Your hobby
turned into a career. A small price to pay
for increased earnings.
How Much Do You Want to Make?
How would you like to buy
4,081 of the world's best minds?
This is the beginning of a bright new future.
There's no substitute for the *right* pliers
when you need it.

ii.
Everyone an inventor. Everybody a patent pending.

Spark plugs. Hair tonic. Transistor radio repair.
A plastic sandwich machine. Cut-out coupons.
The secrets of the ventriloquist revealed. How to
hypnotize your boss. How to build your own helicopter,
and fly it. How to grow two inches with a good pair
of shoes. How to grow a midget tree. How to break
into anything. Develop a he-man's voice in the privacy
of your own home. Geiger counter kits. Suede jackets.
Pellet guns. Binoculars and telescopes that can see
forever. False teeth. Floor wax. Shorthand. Barbells.
Charles Atlas, gleaming on the beach. Accounting
courses by mail. Blast-proof buildings. Bird harnesses.
Electric crib rockers. Power tools. The clean cut
of X-Acto knives.

Everyone has the chance to create something
out of nothing.

Outside the Liquor Store

the leaning man rests
elbows propped on newspaper box
wine-soaked T-shirt
laughing belly, cooled by wind.

A weathervane pointing to the sea.

The leaning man despises the arrogance of standing
the sober snub of a nose in air
the upright posture
denying he ever swung through trees.

Yet, he refuses to live on his back.
Isn't going down without a fight.
So he leans.

Knows exactly which way
he's headed.

Falling for a Glacier

We rest along a moraine
watch shadows crawl
across a glacier.
Jimmy Durante smokes
a cigar in a crevasse.
It's actually Jimmy Durante, we say.
A spider web drifts by
the holy glint of sun.

A young family startles our solitude,
stops at the river below.
Father rests boot on boulder
fingers on chin, preaches a sermon
on family values. We worry
we should be doing something
other than loafing & laughing:
sweep scree from trails
uncover fossils that tell us who we are.
On their way back, mother herds
children onto the path.

Keep walking, she whispers.

Sky darkens. Swollen rain
splatters our world. We huddle
beneath stunted spruce,
the gentle faith of alpine meadows.
Glacier, drunken blue. Waterfall slurring.
Even crows sound like loons.

Everything shimmering
with the weight
of rain.

Mountains Eclipsed by Curtains

He speaks about flowcharts and becoming alive. The
collective wisdom of clams. How many clouds fit into sky.
How we wet our pants when we read aloud. "Another
pink sheet is coming," he says. Each t and p popped into
the mic, the sputtering rattle of lips, teeth, and heavy
breathing. We wince as the busboy pans for gold
and shuffles another bucket of cutlery. Beside me, my
dead father butters a bun, brushes crumbs from the
tablecloth, and makes a loud swallowing sound.

We become distracted by the intimacy of whispering into
each other's ears. The ice cubes hiss in the water glass.
Only seven hours to go.

"Open your binders," he says. "Let's get started."

Ganga Goes Home

Holy men say that Brahma
placed it
there
to hold holy water
drained from the Himalayas
to quench thirst
to wash our sins away,
its current carrying ashes
to a better life.

For thousands of years
Ganga meandered and flowed
the way timeless rivers do.

One day
much to everyone's surprise
the river Ganges got up
and walked away.

It wasn't a lunge or rush of speed
to beat a red light.

It was a gradual movement.
An old woman pushing herself up
from a chair
to put on a kettle.
The soundless breath
of a monk in meditation.

Mother Ganga slowly retreated
from poisons pumped into her
from riverside factories, raw sewage, acid rain
and abuse, from those who claim
to love and worship her.

As calmly as she first came,
she packed up her river beds
and ambled
back into the hills.

The Undoing of Doing

For 14 days I try to think about nothing
meditate on an eight-armed googly-eyed god
a hairdo of serpents, a necklace
of tiny skulls.
I imagine him at the wheel of an El Camino
racing through Himalayan skies
gnashing his teeth at a flock of vultures
and the soft clouds he passes through.

14 days and I still can't pronounce
Om Mani Padme Hum.

I obsess with hunger, my next bowl of lentils
the sandalwood scent of the Irish girl beside me.
"This is so heavy, man. Don't you just love it?"

Every time I sink into my cushion
I'm distracted by gurgling intestines
ignited by rancid water buffalo
a Himalayan farmer offered
while I was lost along a river.

14 days and I dream of suffering
fever under a sleeping bag
shiver to a bootlegged Smiths' tape on my Walkman,
oh very nice, very nice, very nice,
maybe in the next world

14 days and I think about everything
but nothing
sit on a porch with a monk
stare at the distraction of mountains
every slab of rock in my way.

Courting the Critics

Beneath a waterfall
I sit on a rock
play my bamboo flute
for thirsty flies
licking salt from my skin.

The sun is warm
the breeze cool.
All is good
in our universe

until I smack my hat on a black fly
that tore a tiny chunk from my calf.

The rest scatter
into a different death.

I pick up my flute
serenade an ant
skittering through the hairs
of my leg.

Finally, Some Answers

Imagine the chaos if we could move while dreaming?
Everyone beside you would be dead.
—Michio Kaku

As always, I grab too much toilet paper,
but what's the alternative?
Nothing is as simple as it seems:
e.g. the shoelace. The motion of falling moons.
The dog-slobbered tennis ball.
And what's all this about dark matter?
Once again, we're asked to trust the invisible.
Press buttons we don't fully understand.
Squint at an eye chart, like it's our first time.

E
F P
T O Z

Isn't it enough to interpret an ink blot
as Ukrainian dancers slapping their heels
not a squished cat on the freeway?
Or that we can use "hirsute" in a poem?
As a kid I felt holy gazing at phytoplankton
somersaulting upon the shore at night.
Then a foghorn and everything changed.

At four a.m. the brain surgeon asks my wife
her thoughts on drilling a three-inch hole
into my head. Two weeks later
the Tibetan custodian: "Oh good my friend.
You're not going to die."

All afternoon I've been listening to the radio
and staring at the frozen condensation
inside our kitchen window.
Another jazz legend passes away.

The fridge hums, then quiets.
Then hums again.

For now I'm just happy to drink
eight glasses of water a day.
See my kids walk through the door each night.
Dream about the word abalone
and wake to the woman I love
her deep breath
her warm body disappearing
under blankets.

A Good Window

No matter how your heart may pound
stride forth bravely
stop
stand still like the scourge youth of Africa.
Act as if you loved it.

Imagine the audience owes you money.
Imagine you're a Western Union boy
delivering a message.

If we sit, let us be careful how we sit.
A baby does not cling to chairs
after it learns to walk.
A man's gestures, like his toothbrush
are very personal things.

Learn how to win a point
without making an enemy.
Do not emulate the mountain goat.
Visualize in flaming letters of fire.

Toss chicken bones and olive seeds
over your shoulder.
You pay your host a compliment
when you do that. And he likes it.

Glorified gossip will almost always win
and hold attention.
Our interests swarm about our egos.

Hit one syllable. Hit it hard
and hurry over the others
like a car passing a string of hobos.

Drink long and often. Love your audience.
Eat sparingly as a saint.

A good window does not call attention
to itself. It merely lets in the light
like the 'oo' in booze.

II: Taming Ourselves

We argue over whose nose it has.
When their tight lips curl towards a smile
we tingle with delight.

A Tiny Crack

He spits out tomato sandwich, sprints
to his convertible and races
into the shirtless August sun
in pursuit of a man who spun his wheels
outside our summer cabin, gravel shrapnel
exploding under tires
a tiny crack in our living room window.

He keeps a machete in the trunk
for times like these, my mother says.

Two days later, I wait for my father
on the corrugated mud of low tide.
A plastic bucket in one hand, a metal shovel
in the other. My feet too light
to crease the damp sand.
When he doesn't arrive
and my mother is out of every excuse—
his dead clock battery
the grueling overtime
the charity work at church
she smokes her last cigarette
and futilely digs for crayfish
my bait for the bullhead-derby.
The sad lure of crustaceans
bubbling underfoot.
My mother tears through the earth
searches for what is fleeing
always just out of reach.

That afternoon I dangle my line off the pier
hook camouflaged by a scrap of hotdog.
I imagine my father
swinging a machete out the car window.
Out of gas he sprints through busy streets
knocks pedestrians to the ground

too obsessed with catching the man
to turn around and say, "I'm Sorry."
He leaps across creeks
and a line of cheerleaders
squirming between motorcycle ramps.
Does the machete glisten between his teeth?
Does anyone worry he's not wearing sunscreen?

I pull a bullhead taut along the ruler
painted on the judge's table
take home an Adidas bag for second prize.
There through the kitchen window
my dad tans nude on the back patio.
A glass of white wine
an ashtray

overflowing.

When You Fall in Love with Your Babysitter

Let her be a beauty queen
who drives her Dad's convertible to the beach
blasts The 5th Dimension
through the 8-track
and sings *Aquarius* at the top of her lungs.

When she kisses her boyfriend on the porch
or disappears on the back
of his motorcycle
let it be your first lesson
in the cliché of love:

the heart-crushing-ache of falling
for beauty

the slender door between ethereal and real

your shaky footing on the earth
not so familiar anymore.

Let her tuck you in at night.
Dream about a kiss on the cheek.
Hope you're so adorable
she won't let go.

No Shame in a Navel

Even at eleven, I knew something was wrong.
Not fooled by the illusion of laugh track
nor blinded by the haughty charm
and freshly pressed pyjamas of Major Nelson.

I wanted to fly to Cape Canaveral.
Uncork her bottle.
Insist she wouldn't have to call me *Master*.
Save her the humiliating tic-like blink of an eye.
I'd do dishes. Vacuum shag. Wax the Firebird.
Vow she wouldn't get in trouble for being curious.

I'd unveil the scoundrel Larry Hagman became.
Warn her never to trust the bumbling best friend.
Stick a hose in the nosy neighbour's mail slot.
Declare how cute she looks hidden in a cup
full of pencils.

It would be hard at first:
I'd get an extra paper route.
Live in the bottle when things got rough.
Summon her magic if it meant missing a meal.
Cover her in down during Canadian winters.

I know my parents would love her.

But at times, if her glance missed mine
I'd wonder: is she really happy?
Is she dreaming of him and his Cheshire grin?
The two of them weightless
floating above the moon

flashing her forbidden belly button
to the world.

Winter Tires in My Father's Trunk

Her neighbours, tired
of falling asleep, become spectators
in our lives.

A family in the upstairs apartment
prop elbows on window ledge, rest heads
in sleepy palms
and gawk at my mother's hands
bruised from banging on his mistress' door.

It's winter. She needs her tires.

I believe if I cry, "*Fuck Off!*"
they will close the blinds
and return to their dreams.

In the morning they might recall
getting up
for a glass of water, the misty hue
of police lights
splashing through puddles

the siren scream of a nine-year-old
just wanting to go home.

Still Life: It's Hard Letting Go

i.
My *'Keep on Truckin'* t-shirt world
has changed forever.

I've discovered James Bond
saving the planet, squeezing through neon nights
of Vegas, dropping dice with Plenty O'Toole
blocking barefoot blows from Bambi
and Thumper.

I sleuth through our house with a walkie-talkie
and plastic black Beretta
each room an exotic continent.
I dazzle Moneypenny with my youthful wit and charm.
Take my juice shaken, not stirred.

Cardboard-boxed treasures in dark corners
of our basement: abandoned corporate letterhead
years of tattered Playboys
Hawaiian doll in grass skirt, a little hula dance
every time I give her head a flick.

I discover a clandestine envelope marked "Confidential":
a couch and television receipt from a furniture store
in the desert, a thousand miles
from our damp home.
A faded Polaroid labeled top secret:
my dad in his rat-pack glory
laughing, his arm around a young brunette
under the cool shade of a Sammy Davis Jr. marquee.

As a spy in her majesty's secret service
I travel upstairs to my mom,
reveal my evidence.

Watch her cry.

ii.
What a lover she must have been.
On the third day following my father's death
there she is again–thirty-one years later–
as I clean out the top shelf of his golf club locker
anonymous among scattered tees
buried under a highball glass of matchbooks.

Young, snazzy 8 by 10 lovers, arm in arm
at a showroom table in the Sands Hotel.

He's got the world by the tail.

Even now, she looks young, beautiful
unfazed by his passing.

Shallows by the Shore

My sons build an island of sand. I'm reminded of
a New Yorker cartoon: shipwrecked people, longing
for something: a witty punch line, a last regret,
a coconut shell SOS.

They shovel with glee. Drown thirst with juice boxes.
Rest in the water and float like tiny miracles.

Their mom drifts by on a mattress, lulled by sun
and waves. A trout, bored with water lunges on the back
of a passing butterfly. In Cuba, a small fishing boat
capsizes.

The boys shovel until there is no longer island nor lake.
Just a sad stretch of land cooled by a hovering glacier.

A developer stakes the ground with the swagger
of someone about to cannonball in a public pool.
The local beauty queen is wistful—
knows she'll never houseboat in the lake again,
never celebrate her victory
under a shower of crackling stars.

At night, everyone pretends to sleep, yet when they
touch each other, it's as if they're feeling a door to test
for fire on the other side.

In the morning, we return to the spot that was once
a shore. The boys dig. A pool of water percolates up
through sand.

They leap in, see who can make the biggest splash
and swim for miles under the blue thing they call sky.

Quantum Humour

Mystics envision a laugh
a deep infinite belly roar.

Skeptics suggest a sneeze
a sudden splatter of matter
one quickly regrets.

Scientists profess two lonely universes
innocently brushed elbows
in the awkward elevator of the cosmos.

My eight-year-old kneels at his window
beside me
gazes at the night sky
ponders the infinite, gets frustrated
trying to fathom the unfathomable.

"I hate it," he says, the universe
not fitting into his concrete world.

Later in bed he laughs into his pillow
surrenders the search for a punch line
finally sees the vast humour
of it all.

One Tooth Wiser

Beneath the sleepy weight of your head
I tuck a loonie under your pillow
feel my way in night-lite darkness
for the note you left, asking the tooth fairy
to leave the tooth if she doesn't mind.
You want to show your mom and friends:
A miniature ivory trophy
you parade between your fingers.

I listen for your deep-sleep breathing
and sneak downstairs, one creak at a time.
Fifteen minutes later
my hands in warm dishwater
you are in the kitchen
giggling with a coin in your hand
asking for a glass of water
barely able to swallow
you're laughing so hard.

I ask, "What are you laughing at?"
"I saw you. I waited up and saw you!" you confess
one tooth wiser.

At five a.m. I'm awoken by you running into our room
showing us the dollar the tooth fairy left you.
I smile
and rub your back.
We drift off into hopeful dreams.

After Reading a Bedtime Story to My Son

I sit at my desk to write a poem, gaze out the window,
put down my pen and smile. "Hello, Chestnut tree," I say.
"Hello, Mark Creek. Hello, tree whose leaves are turning
reddish." I shake my head, smile again. "Hello, power lines
in the dark distance." I rest my pen on a pad of yellow
paper. Thirty faint blue lines, and not a word written.
I close my eyes, quiet my thoughts. "Hello, empty mind,"
I say. I think about the silence of windshield wipers
at night. The wee gasp of barnacles when the tide
recedes. How pasta can be made into 600 shapes.
I open my eyes, drawn to top left corner of the window.
"Hello, tiny crack."

It Would Be Easier

if he stopped at just one stone. Or a handful.
But he is six, and determined to rid the riverbank
of every rock, stick and last grain of sand.

Nothing is beyond him.

He runs to the shore, flings rocks into the river
a victory with every splash.

When the beach is empty
he moves to trees, then RV's. Frying pans
and outhouses. Fire pits smeared with marshmallows.
Everything goes in: a rusty bus, a roadside hot dog stand,

a merry-go-round of airplanes. A lost button.
An adult video store. A horizon of skyscrapers.

He tears mountains from their roots and heaves them
into the river. Plucks clouds from the sky and chokes
them under water. Tosses Australia in the air
like pizza dough.

All dragged downstream.

The last smug cockroach thrashes on his back.
Not a fleck of dust caught in the sun.

Just him, brushing his hands.
Grinning.

Taming Ourselves

Evolution is one mistake after another.
—Dean Young

Who can resist their bulging, blinking eyes?
The way they hug a branch, hurl a hungry
tongue towards a fly. We fawn over
how they lock their bones
still their breath, pretend to be a twig—
their silly green skin mutating to brown.
We stuff our wallet with their image.
Tack them to our cubicles at work.

We tire of the greedy way they devour mice.
Bully & beg for a bag of crickets.
Their cold distant stare, longing for the days
of everything volcanic.
They'd gnaw our flesh
clean from the bone
if it weren't for their puny jaws.

We coax them from cages, from slimy plastic pools.
Bribe them with shiny carrots
and waxed apple skins fresh from the market.
Perched on our shoulders
we parade them through parks.
Hold staring contests during long car rides.
Let them burrow into the shag carpet
as we tear into TV dinners.
How they love their scaly spines
rubbed before bedtime.

We tug at their tiny arms till they're extinct.
Praise them when they arch their backs
teeter on two feet. We oil cracked skin.
Wipe food from chins.
Sleep with one eye open, await a choke, a sputter

or a first word.
We argue over whose nose it has.
When their tight lips curl towards a smile,
we tingle with delight

and pray that one day
they'll be exactly
like us.

III: Closest Thing to a Love Poem

Arguments over silly things
we thought defined ourselves

The Empathy of Opposites

We analyze data regarding the caution
of moving forward. Discuss the thoughtful
overlap of ideas. How anxious ravens
peck at roadkill.

We research the trick of hiding things
we can't hold together.
The liturgy of light.
The slipstream of birds.
The tenderness of diagrams.

We award points for breathing.
Check boxes. Plot behaviours.
Adjust schedules.
Keep an eye on each other.
Gamble on the eventual.

If not for love
we'd be onto something.

I Lost My Hand

Left it on your ass last night
when I fell asleep.
Yes, there it is.
That's my ring. That's my scar
from the neighbour's dog.

It's been awkward for me:
the nervous glances of children,
sympathetic comments from strangers,
"You poor thing. You're missing a hand."
The thorny glare from those missing two hands.

I can't imagine what people say to you.

I hope it's not too inconvenient.
The panty lines. The way you're forced
to lean when you sit.
The discomfort while standing on a crowded bus.

Yet at night I roll onto my stomach, reach
my arm over to you, reattach my hand
and tighten my grip
until the severed light of morning
tears us apart again.

Smoke Rings with Margaret Atwood

Most mornings, we sat on the porch in pajamas
shared a cigarette and stared at clouds.
"Nice sky," she'd say, looking at something
only she could see.

Toward the end of the month
before her next cheque arrived, I'd make her coffee.
She'd offer advice on writing, our feet resting
on the railing: "Try the Halibut at Saunders.
Next time, how 'bout a little less sugar."
After coffee, we'd share a smoke.
She'd take a long pull, ash and cherry crackling
towards her fingers. "Check this out," she'd say.

For years I watched her jam her tongue towards
the back of her throat, contort her mouth
into a coin-shaped O, these tiny bursts
of smoke pulled towards the sky.
I despised the sound of her choking,
how she poked at these ragged shapes
she confused for circles.

Once she told me to open a banana
from the bottom end.
A real breakthrough.
At month-end, I gave notice.

Never saw her again.

Nothing Between Us That Is Not Love

We flee south across the border
into our quiet conversation.
Feet on dash, yawning August sun, a CD on repeat.
I cry for the first time in years.
Something I heard in a song.
Something about not wanting to lose you.
The twenty-four years of *Where to from here?*

We ignore the distractions of the unfamiliar:
the quivering shadows cast from tinsel hung in a bar
a flea-market veteran selling switchblades from China
a Baptist church's hay-baled pews.

There is a lawn mower race.
Huckleberry pancakes in a diner.
We wrestle poems onto napkins:
the anonymous graffiti of bathroom stalls
black and white beauty-queen photos
the arrogant chit-chat of Libertarians
beside us.

It always comes down to this: How long do we hold on?

The windshield's cake batter of bugs. All this ends.
Every poem, every argument, says run like hell.
Yet we grip hands
wobble through town as one
then retreat to our hotel room in the late afternoon
afraid to let go.

At the lakeside Wilco concert, the evening sun
bounces off trees.
An osprey soars through *The Star-Spangled Banner*.
A middle-aged pirate dances by the speaker.
Alison, beautiful on our blanket, spreads
blue cheese on crackers.

The intimate act of passing things without saying a word.

When the band stops, we holler words
that would sound strange in a bank.
In the confusion of an encore, we stumble
over beach chairs, slip past an angry security guard.
At the stage, we join the frenzy
feel the futility of stomping on soft grass.
The hope of something more.

Something that never ends.

Things We Don't Know

Madonna deals blackjack at the Imperial Palace.
Flicks me cards like she's drying her nails.

I'm losing every hand.

Every time she wins, she winces
like I've pissed away our kids' college fund.
On 14, I hit an 8, and she pouts
her anatomy sagging towards the floor.
When I stay on 13, she hits a five-card 21.
She lowers her head, and if I was sober
I would see the beginning of a tear
before she chokes it off.

She will sell a kidney on EBay,
toe clippings to Satanist conventioneers.
She will give her tiny red dress to a divorcee from Miami
and stuff breakfast sausages from the buffet
into her cleavage.

When Elvis arrives to relieve her
she floats to a tiny stage
turns down her mic
and lip-synchs something sad about our love:

how when we try to win
we lose so much of each other.

Fasten Your Seatbelt

I look at the empty seat
to my left and imagine
if this plane
were to snap in two
contents scattered into sky

I would want you
next to me
holding hands
falling together
towards snow covered peaks.

I'd gather bags of peanuts
tiny bottles of wine
and prepare for landing.

When Told to Leave

you do what's familiar.
What instinct dictates.
Scoop bundles of clothes
on hangers. Heap them onto the bed.
Wonder if there's an iron where you're going.

You marvel at the certainty of clichés:

a screaming wife, the crying kids,
a figurine broken on the ground.
You grab car keys, unsure where you're going.

A friend? A relative? A dark patch of road?
Sammy Davis Jr. offering a lift in his T-bird?
You land in an empty bar.

Lip-read baseball highlights.
Line up straws on the table
one for each rye through your liver.

Were you hoping the waitress would save you?
Invite you to her place? Introduce her 6-year-old?
You drive home, pray the doors aren't locked.

A note on the kitchen table:
I'm not giving up on us.

You crawl to the basement.
Listen to the sobs upstairs.
You fall asleep.

You dream.

Here We Are in Bed Again

the two of us
rigid as corpses.
If someone filmed our sleep
camera on ceiling
we'd appear to be standing
the mattress a tattered wall
the Rolling Stone
a crumpled poster.

People on their way to work
would mistake us for complete strangers
arms crossed, tight faces.

The newspaper boy speeding past on his bike
would tell his mom about the dog that almost bit him
and these two sad people
who just missed their bus.

But we are asleep
so close, I can almost touch you.
Our dead relatives above us.
The sleepy thud of our bodies.

How greedy our lungs for air.

She's the Kind of Girl

who stares at the shivering sky
whispers, "I don't like the colour of Mars."
Adoring men, attempt to do something about it.

The impulsive wrap tinfoil around their arms
spray-paint cardboard helmets silver
fly to Florida and hijack space shuttles.

The patient enroll in first-year physics
spend endless nights on calculators and slide rulers
wake with fistfuls of hair.

The sly tinker in dark basements on gleaming machines
create things they might have seen in sci-fi films.
A washing machine fused to a furnace.
A rocket that won't fit through the door.

Some imagine her blind, convincing her
that indeed the colour has changed.
"If only you could see it," they say.

All crazy as bulls
staring at this angry red planet.

She Wears Him Down

When she struts by
she touches him, just enough
so he doesn't feel her
yet a tiny piece
of him
wears away.
Skin.
Molecules.
Even the infinite space between atoms
flee for something gentler.

A black hole. An exploding star.

At night, she is less subtle.
She files away whole parts.
"Tonight, a toe," she says, and labours
into the wee hours.

She uses emery cloth and sandpaper
to shape him
so if someone walks in
he'll blend into the fold
of her sheets.

As if she sleeps alone.

The Breakfast We Never Shared

It was late and you drank
too much
to call a cab
your dog and cat barking—
meowing you home.

I look around this empty kitchen.
You're worse than a memory.

The eggs colder without you.
The coffee bitter.
The conversation flat:
Where are the Marxists today?
Who will catch on fire?
What extremes must we endure
to keep the line moving?

Even the water tastes stale.
The glare of snow so pushy.
The sun, no consolation
for this lonely winter.

On my stereo in the living room
Dean Martin croons

> *Return to me*
> *Return to me.*

The Closest We Come to Touch

We sit on the bathroom floor.
Pick through our hair for lice.

Crash into each other doing dishes.
Sidestep the shrapnel of cutlery.

Our morning goodbye: lips pinched.
Two skulls kissing.

We make love like drunk dogs.
Whimper off to our corners.

Flinch in our sleep.
Dreamily mistake a kick for a cuddle.

We settle for these tender moments.
Ache at how our love evolved.

The Heart Aches

On a brain scan, romantic love
resembles addiction.

He fell asleep after her
hypnotized with how her toes held up the sheets.

They made love before the kids woke up
then fell asleep. He struggled for the snooze alarm
his arm trapped by the drowsy weight of her head.

When the current of longing hurts too much
they reach for each other.

A kiss of light. A flash.
A spark
six times hotter

than the surface of the sun.

What's Left to Say?

She scolds you to drink up.
Spits your name like a torn fingernail
when you ask for another.

It's not really your name
yet you want to believe her.

You imagine your parents imagining you.
The hopeful list of names—
Movie stars. Musicians. Politicians.
Hip names they chant like mantras.
Yet the morning you were born
they scratch out every name but one:
the boring uncle who died six times in the war
and returned to boast about it,
his cold cut cheeks stuffed with holidays.

"Barmaid, I'd like another," you say.

She splashes a last call look in your eyes
like she's never been called barmaid
and hollers your counterfeit name
over the drunken drumroll of scattered coins.
Although she's kicking her way to the door
you sip your tired drink.

You are a stranger.
You are you again.
You never left.

He Loved so Hard

The first night they met at a party
he braced his drunken self against a doorjamb.
"So, am I staying at your place tonight?
We don't have to do anything.
We can just sleep beside each other."

He loved so hard on their first date
he took her to the fluorescent glare of Zellers
watched her wander down the aisles.
A bathmat. A can opener. Something to write with.
The next day, he mailed her a Zellers card
a short poem, wild flowers
he picked along the dump road.

He loved so hard
that every time he missed an opportunity
to open a door
shave when going out on a date
lay a coat over a muddy puddle
or rescue her from some tall tower
he wished they'd never invented television
or fly fishing
or toenails that needed to be clipped
at the dinner table.

He loved so hard
after 24 years of hospital beds and parents' deaths
and the things we say but can never take back
he wanted her more every day.
Thought she looked more beautiful
stronger, wiser
than the night he met her.

He loved her so hard
he wanted to be a part of her dreams
but knew he could have done a better job
getting the part.

He loved so hard
he thought if he could do things all over
he might lean into a doorjamb at a party
casually mention something he heard
on Peter Gzowski that morning:
how a bug flies into a candle
mistakes it for the moon, and stars.
That this is a clear pathway.

Everything is going to be OK.

Still, I Find Myself Missing You

Still, I find myself missing

Still, I find myself

Still, I find

Still, I

Still.

Closest Thing to a Love Poem

"Ten years and you've never written me
a love poem," you say
in the greying light of fall.

I think, but don't say
our love has been lost in the mundane
moments of family life. In laundry loads
and sleepless nights. Arguments over silly things
we thought defined ourselves.

Not forever gone, but like salt mixed
in warm water. One must look
so hard

to see it.

IV: BEFORE THE FIRST POEM

floating in the ether
bouncing off waves.
Elusive and playful.
Sacred and still.

Surprised by Bukowski

The first time I met him
he asked about my mortgage rate
and if I ever tried nutmeg cream sauce.

I steered him back to the ponies
and how life can beat the hell outta ya.

I asked him the best way to hit a man
when a guy should stay down, or take a powder.
He babbled on about mindfulness
how he enjoys gardening, and yerba mate.
Before I left, he told me to breathe
and not take life so seriously.

Driving home, the sun
was so bright
I could barely see
the fucking
smog.

Sleeping with bill

we sleep inside each other all
-bill bissett

I sleep under your paintings
in a hotel room overlooking English Bay.
Walls adorned with universes of you:
yellow skies explode in naked throats
mountains erupt beneath shoulder blades
watery blue birds coo in your lungs.

I awake at dawn. A restless poem
flapping in the wind, one corner
chopping at the desktop
another held down
by Gertrude Stein's *Tender Buttons*.

The poem is about you.
The boundless ways you are loved.
Each poem a love song, a sublime scripture
like all poems scattered throughout this room.

I rest my feet on the window ledge
light a cigarette and capsize a sleepy freighter
under my big toe. A seagull sails by
turns toward me
caught by the our swirling energy
fed by wind and last night's dreams.
It scrapes the concrete ledge, inches from my feet
peers in like someone
late for a plane while visiting a gallery.
It pokes its head under the window
pecks at the ashtray
and vanishes with a butt.

I feel the bite of the bay breeze
and close the windows.
The room slips into the sounds
of a waking city muted.
And the poem with tender wings folds itself
atop Gertrude Stein
shields her
from the morning light.

the day bill bissett blew into town

          people appeared like curious crop circles
              forgot most earthly conventions
    how 2 spel, keep trak uv time, th wet lawndree
            still in th dryer
                 no wun cud xplayn th suddn urge
                       2 hug eech othr.

The day bill bissett blew out of town
people soberly went back about their business
unpacked dictionaries, set watches
made neat starched creases in their clothes
yet when they looked in mirrors

               thay saw brillyant smyles
                  nevr seen b4

Only Fools Go to All That Work

Bukowski didn't dream
of being a writer.
He dreamt he'd pretend
to be a writer.

He'd follow the landlady's ass upstairs.
Screw all day.
Smoke her cigarettes.
Eat cast iron stew.

Sure I'm a writer, he'd slur.

Never write
just pretend.

Life would be
a helluva lot easier.

Searching for bill bissett

In Chapters, a kind-faced bearded man
in a red vest searches for bill.
He mutters, *"He's the fellow who never capitalizes, isn't he?"*
and leads me through the crisp aisles.
He scans the meagre Canadian poetry section.
*"Nope. Doesn't look like we have any.
Lots of Leonard Cohen though."*

Google bill bissett and you get 14,800 entries.
11,000 are for an accountant in Windsor.

I youtubed bill today.
Jacqueline Bissett appeared in a clip
to the tune, *You're so Damn Beautiful.*
In each image, she aged gracefully
though nothing like the first time I saw her
mouth open wide, slithering
through the sea in a tight white T-shirt.

There are 800 Jacqueline Bissett youtube clips.
19 of bill bissett.
Maybe bill needs to swim underwater in a T-shirt
let his nipples hum Phil Collins tunes
a whale searching for its young.

In the Indian restaurant's fish tank
there is no sign of bill
but outside, in the summer sky
a cloud resembles Jon Bon Jovi.
And if you squint
it looks more like bill
than a cloud
much lighter
and less scary
when you fly a plane through it.

On Bukowski's Last Beating

he didn't make a sound.

His father, terrified by silence
never struck him again.

Never realized a razor strop

made such an awful thwack.
The drip in the bathroom sink

deafening.

Breakfast with bill at the Sylvia Hotel

I gaze through ocean windows
at the sand jaywalking across Beach Ave.
Our weathered waitress applies lipstick
stares into a compact, dabs corners
of her mouth with a pinky.
She's making a game out of ignoring us.
bill's not bothered.

He eats peanut butter from tiny plastic squares
and takes an orange from his bag.
I ask him about something, without really
remembering what it was. He says, *"i dont no.
cant yu say that abt evereething?"*

Suddenly, police barricade the street.
Either we're in trouble
or someone important is coming
like the president, or Anne Murray.
Instead, a huge congregation emerges
and dances towards us.
bill says, *"letz go 2 th terrus nd investigayte."*

Outside there's chanting and drums for Krishna.
A beautiful helium awning with a guru
carried by devotees. The waitress
blinks in the sun and says, *"Well, will you look at that."*
After they pass, everybody seems more peaceful.
Even downtown traffic is honking less.

When we return to the table, our waitress appears
like an old friend. She calls bill, *"Sweety."*

Before leaving, bill gives a poem
to an elderly man in a suit who looks puzzled
yet touched

then returns to his newspaper—
something about mortgage rates
the falling price of oil

how nobody can afford anything.

Before the First Poem and After the Last

Before ballads born in sleepy, mud-walled towns
and tranquil haiku brushed.
Long before two roads diverged in the woods.

Before Dylan raged
and Krishna sung
slams begun
and rappers spun.

Before nursery rhymes
and babies fell out of trees.
Before Jack and Jill felt thirsty.

Before Webster's and words
caveman walls
and bathroom stalls.

Before bissett chanted
and Bukowski slurred.

Before metaphors and magical mystery tours.

Before a morning dew
or a moonlit night.
A lover's gaze
and bad clichés.

Before the crash of a car or the boom of a bomb.
Before anyone had the balls
to spell onomatopoeia.

Before the paradox of parables
and a camel through a needle's eye.
Before amoeba dreams
and God Save the Queen.

Long before the first infant poem

floating in the ether
bouncing off waves.

Elusive and playful.

Sacred and still.

V: One Dies One's Life

Every morning driving to work
I observe the same retired couple
scurry past the graveyard.

Things Get Progressively Worse

In the beginning a dull pain.
A throb. A wince. A mild fever.
In the grocery store the cashier
raves about her cat and laughs
at my swollen cheek. *You should suck
on cloves*, she suggests.

Then a mass shooting in San Bernardino.

An eavestrough bloated with snow
tears from our house. An astronaut
floating in space glares at the camera
like a hostage warned not to speak.
Get me the hell out of here.
My sister sounds hurt when I forget
her birthday. A plane is shot down.
Even the neighbour's arthritic Lab
limps to our porch and slips on the stairs.

Remember the mobster who threatened
Tony Montana to stay clear of champagne
and chicks? He died today.
And my daily horoscope? *Whatever happens,
keep telling yourself it's not as bad
as it seems.* If I were a Leo, today holds
great romantic potential. At a climate
summit, Robert Redford warns
*Glaciers are melting quicker than any time
in the last 2,000 years.*

And just when things can't get any worse
a tissue I'd left in a pocket
explodes in the dryer. On the nightly news
the US announces they've increased air
strikes in Syria. Three days on the couch
and I'm barely able to eat a grape.

At the Turkish border a Syrian father
stumbles as he tries to lift his daughter
strapped into a wheelchair. Soon
he will start to cry.

I'm told ice, Advil, the occasional shot
of whiskey, and things might improve
by tomorrow.

When You Walk Through Walls

The first
step
always
the hardest.

One Foot Out

He lived life in similes
never really in a moment
without comparing it
to another. Unaware
of the lethal nature
of clichés.

"I'm working like a dog," he'd say.
"Smoking like a chimney."
Tiny grey clouds backfiring
from his lips
with each new syllable.

He drank like a fish.

And died
like

he lived.

Bridge to the Afterlife

My father's dying. The clues: his bloated, taut skin.
The rhythm of machines. The concerned look of nurses
working overtime, draining pus pooling in tubes.

In his garage 14 cases of Chardonnay
two weeks overdue for bottling.

They will close Lions Gate Bridge
so he can transfer to St. Paul's.
He's the guy in the ambulance bystanders wonder about.

My family will get kicked out of the waiting room
drunk on rye, asking an intern for more ice.

On Christmas Eve I will retreat to my bed.
Say goodbye over the phone. Sit with my son
in my lap, light candles and incense.
Wait for the phone call to come.

He's gone.

The image that recurs is the man in the grey sedan
stuck in rush hour on Lions Gate Bridge.
His angry eyes
grab mine speeding past.

He would eagerly trade places
with my dad, just to get where he's going
faster.

The Audacity of Aging

At 50, everyone has the face he deserves.
—George Orwell

One day, we wake up and realize
we're too old to search for the drunken shoes
of missing friends. Too old to translate
their late-night babblelogue slurring
towards the door. Too old to lean against
the sink at three a.m. and wash hi-ball
glasses inherited from my father.
Each one a frosted map of Florida,
and other places he dreamt about.

Yet we're still invited to parties
of a younger crowd
navigating the precarious window
before we resemble their parents.
Before they hand us their clinging kids
and bedtime storybooks.
"Liam likes his back scratched," they will say.

In five years we'll call the police,
complain about the brouhaha next door
the hipster parents playing bocce at midnight
their hissing meat spitting at our fence.

We notice how quiet we've become.

We tiptoe into their homes, pause
inside the doorway, kick snow from our boots
like fuddy-duddies in galoshes and hairnets.
In the living room, a young father is surrounded
by a ring of clapping people.
He's doing The Swim.
He plugs his nose, bloats his cheeks
and submerges beneath the surface.
He wiggles his hips, as if to deceive the water

into letting him in.
Now he's a sprinkler.
Now a robot.
Now he's twerking.
And although I've never hit anyone

I want to slug him.

I want to retreat home
and watch Ed Sullivan introduce the Beatles.
But in the kitchen, there are beautiful women
in Asian dresses. On the counter
a cheese tray
adorned with parsley.

Separated at Death

A human brain rests in a 3.7% formaldehyde solution
on a classroom shelf. The label on its Plexiglas case:
HUMAN HALF BRAIN, Right Hemisphere. It was
purchased in 1971 from the Carolina Biological Supply
Company. You can no longer buy a human half brain.
A plastic replica retails for $540. My seven-year-old son
is fascinated by the brain. In the evening, he and his friends
navigate the hallway under the red hue of an EXIT sign.
They sneak up on the brain and giggle nervously.
My four-year-old saw it only once. He dreams about
the brain. Its arterial veins purple, stained with blood.
Its fat Chinese noodles huddled in fetal position.
Over 4,000 students have examined the brain.
Many ask if they can hold it. Some shake it gently.

A Universe. A Day.

i.
Alison scrambles eggs and fries
a pound of bacon for the boys.
She scrapes the Teflon pan
with a metal spatula.
A robin considers crashing into our window
but changes her mind.
Alison never uses a metal spatula.
After we clean up breakfast
she takes a photo from her mom's childhood album.
She says, "I'm not very good with numbers.
It's my mother's birthday.
I wonder how old she'd be?"

ii.
The sun shivers behind a cirque.
A tower of ice tears from a glacier
our lake-calm capsized by a panicked wave
that screams towards our canoe.
The boys alone on shore, keys hidden
in the bumper.
As the wave approaches
we imagine surfing its crest
thrown to a treetop
clinging like wet laundry
a helicopter sputtering above.

But after the last echo of fear
washes ashore
there's barely a ripple.
Just us, gripping the canoe.
Laughing.

iii.
On the dirt road home
we chase a hysterical deer

leaping through dusty air.
A hush of sunlight
hidden in trees.

iv.
Too tired to sleep, we lie in bed.
The gentle pulse in our hands
our grip tightening with each breath.

The Long Strange Trip

Near the foot of the Great Pyramid
the Grateful Dead—
sound beyond place and time.

At dusk Bob Weir
is covered in mosquitos.
"Welcome to hell," he says.
Just then something flies by his face.
The stage is swarmed with bats
taking out mosquitos
saving their asses.

A rock 'n' roll band rages
on a thousand-year-old stage
surrounded by a cloud of bats.

Bob Weir thinks, *Take me now lord*
I wanna remember it
just like this.

The Dead Ant in the Cereal Box

The joy it must have felt
tumbling
into sugary depths
the effortless dark descent.

Lounging in a corner of crumbs
too giddy to carry
a single grain home.

It frolicked and splashed
front legs tucked behind its head
and dreamed it wasn't dreaming.

A few glorious nights
drunk with delight

the tedium of return forgotten.

Ghost Writer

Today I wrote a eulogy
for someone I never met.

He was killed on impact.
His wife in a coma.
His daughter, unscathed, sleeps
on a makeshift cot
at her grandmother's house.

He was a good dancer.
Sang Karaoke, made friends
on the Bow River
where his dog fetched sticks.

Once he lit a menu on fire
leaning across a table
to kiss his fiancé.

When his daughter was born
he was first to hold her

the last to let go.

Thrift Store Counter

"Where'd you get that?" she asked
pointing to a western shirt I was buying.

She folded it neatly, chipped away
at dried oatmeal on the collar.
"Men's shirt," I replied.

"I thought you'd been through
my husband's closet," she said.
"He's been dead five years.

But don't you worry.
We'll be all right.

We'll be all right."

Here I Am

for Bets McKay

We gathered in your living room
days before you died
this intimate place of goodbyes.
You chewed ice chips by the window
sat with heating pads on your feet
told us how you want to return
as a loon.

You choked back tears
when you spoke of letting down the boys
and the things you'll miss most:
baking cookies, cold arenas, picking clothes up
off the floor.
And perhaps things you thought
but too private to mention:
how a canoe veers off course
when paddled alone, a hand in a furry glove
never as warm as when held
by the one you love.

I wanted to hug you
and say something stupid
about the great life you've lived.
Instead I gave you the thumbs up
told you to *hang in there*.

On the way out
my eyes so clouded with tears
I backed into a tree.

Grand Gestures

The day Eddie Mountain died
geese flew south for winter.
The first truck drove across the frozen lake.
A train broke down outside town.

Eddie's wife waited six hours
before calling the ambulance.
She held his hand in the gentle light of dusk
told him everything she forgot to say.

The mayor eulogized Eddie
spoke of his great contributions to the community:
the countless pancakes he flipped
the raffle tickets sold outside
the liquor store.

How will we survive without him?

Twenty-five years later
a young boy in a hockey arena
asked his dad,
"Why do they call the egg sandwich
The McEddie?"

In the Line of Duty

His friends come to my office
tell me he cuts his wrists
his dad beats him
he wants to kill himself.

Only six days till Christmas
and I'm onstage
in 50 minutes to impersonate
Whitney Houston
in front of 400 students.

I call him out of class.
He bares his scarred wrists.
Says his dad hits him.
Kicks him.
Throws him to the floor.
He thinks of suicide.
Knows where all the guns are kept.

His chin quivers, "I know he still loves me."

I call Social Services.
Sit quietly with him
until he's ready to get up
splash water on his face
walk into a jam-packed gym
watch me in heels and wig

lip-sync some sad song about love.

Road Prayers

*As you get older, you get to a point where you feel
like you have seen the world end too many times.*
—Joe Wenderoth

i.
Like most mornings I'm late.
Windshield gripped by stubborn frost.
I scrape clear an icy patch
with an expired credit card.
It creeps back
reclaims what I just took away.

I give up, drive to work
my eye pressed to a one-inch clearing
above my dash
bowing before the dangers that lie ahead.

ii.
In a packed Acadian, we drove through the 80s
like we owned the place.

iii.
A skid mark. A farmer's field.
A birth certificate. A scuffed football.
A Conway Twitty tape torn from the car.
A pit in my stomach every time I drive by.

iv.
In the middle of the night, I wake from a dream
and text a friend: *Thanks for driving us over
the cliff, 500 metres to the rocky bottom below.*
He replies, Huh? and I'm too tired to explain.
I'm fixated on the word for that feeling the moment
the car slips over the edge. No turning back.
That moment balancing on a teeter totter
before you thud to the ground.
The word for that.

V.
Never take your eyes off the road
unless you're in a movie.
Then gaze endlessly
at your passenger
someone you love eternally
no matter what or who
gets in the way.

Why the Horses Ran Away

They punch through cracked concrete.
Toss headstones aside
like wet dogs at a tea party.

They whisper tales we mistake for wind.

Our bellies full of Szechuan and cheap beer
we dance beside the dead.
Return plastic carnations to parched vases.
Brush leaves from unmarked graves
of babies, only two days old
too fresh to notice the difference
between heaven and the lake they lay beside.

We're mesmerized by the unknown—
teenagers who light candles in the dark
sip jungle juice and play truth
or dare
by the oldest grave.

So full of life
we wander home
the dirt road
paved with evening sun.
Each heavy
footstep
lighter
than the last.

The Summer Everything Burnt

Forests were the first to go
then metals, dirt and language.
Insults exploded on lips.
Flash burns left ugly scars. Finally
we started speaking nicely to each other.

As the haze thickened
fire swelled towards sky.
We lost track of the moon,
the sun, the North Star.

With feathers and rattles
we grabbed strangers in the streets
to dance and chant for rain.

Yet a strange thing happened.

Despite the fire's wild wandering
people slowed down, lost
in the hypnotic passage of time.
They made campfire confessions
gazed into flames
mesmerized by dragons, waterfalls
and dead movie stars.

The summer everything burnt
people danced on coals
and forgave what they loved most

floated to the sky like vestal embers.

Small Planet. Big Wave.

Each step.
Each last breath.
Each sunrise swallowed.

A family gathers by the shore.
Offers rose petals to the moon
their feet cool in the mourning sand.

A boy in his grandfather's grip
breaks free, laughs and gathers fish
marooned at the ocean's edge.

By the pool, away from breakwaters
and beach balls
a last coffee.
Crumbs from a croissant.
A waiter glares over
a hedge.

A fisherman drags his boat to shore.
Squats in the sand. Lights his last smoke.

Smiles at his basket full
of gasping fish.

One Dies One's Life

*One is still what one is going to cease to be
and already what one is going to become.
One lives one's death, one dies one's life.*
—Jean-Paul Sartre

Sartre's birthday according to the disc jockey
on the car radio.

I imagine the two of us growing up together.
Me delivering a wooden toy

racing to blow out the candles before him.
In later years we smoke Gauloises
and drink gallons of Bordeaux
until we've forgotten
who we are.

Yet I never knew Sartre nor studied him at college.

Every morning driving to work
I observe the same retired couple
scurry past the graveyard.

The man in Tilley hat and sturdy shorts
drags his wife along
beyond tombstones and bare trees
determined to cheat death.

I smile and wave.

They never return the gesture.

Today, I pretend not to see them.
I stare dead straight ahead.
They mean nothing.

They never existed.

Durbar Square Disappears

i.

In my office, a 30-year-old photo:
Durbar Square
a hundred dead pigeons
who weren't dead at the time
but are certainly gone now.
I lay on the ground with my camera.
They coo and peck
through cobblestone dirt
escape into morning fog
fly into what we think is forever.

ii.

I sip chai in a tea stall
hypnotized by the water buffalo
being tied to a stake
bucking, defecating
and panicking into death.
The executioner raises an axe
lops off its head
deposits it on a wooden table
surrounded by candles, incense
and the skulls of chickens and goats.

Dragged beside a pile of carcases
it rises to its feet, lunges into an abyss
and crumples onto the street.

I don't eat meat for another seven years.

iii.

We wait hours for the Kumari
to arrive at the palace window
to glance at us like a ghost
the eight-year-old goddess of destruction
whose feet never touch the ground.

30 years later I google her.
Her Kumari Palace
surrounded by ruins
yet untouched by earthquake.
In a photo, she appears at the window.
Looks bored.
Indifferent.
Not a worry in the world.

Dear Death

You are the ambulance wailing outside our house
while I grip my son's hand.
I tell him so many things:
How much I love him and his brother.
Tell your mom she's the most amazing person I know.
Where the winter tires are stored.
The $1,200 in poker winnings
squirreled away in a book in my closet.

Death, you are so comfortable in your skin
so hungry for my clammy hand.

You are the logjam in the river.
The undertow in our tides.
The man in the grey van.

You are the doctor
who can't look my son in the eye.

The Tibetan janitor
mopping the fears beside my bed.
The heartbeat monitor chanting
through the night.

Dear Death: you brace my head
in the ambulance.
Crank up the laughing gas
as we slide through the Rockies.
Blast the Black Keys on the stereo,
lip-sync the words with my wife.

I am black ice drunk on you
hungover
regretting the day you laid eyes on me.

Dear Death: why did you break my ThighMaster?
Why are you playing bongos on Granville Street?

You are the bully in the bar
whose eyes I avoid.
You are Andrea Ironside, the girl in grade six
I was too scared to dance with.

Dear Death: why did you invite
the entire class to your party?
Why force them to play musical chairs?

Dear Death: you rip the roof from our homes.
Burn flesh from our bones.
Burst our clotted dams.
Is that you snoring in my bed
counting my breaths on your fingertips?

With my dad clutched in your grip
we drank rye in the hospital lobby
tossed out for making too much noise.

Dear Death: *You make my heart sing.*
You make everything groovy.

You are cliché. A lonely foghorn.
A siren in a rainy night. A bare tree in winter.
The snow-muffled bark of a dog.
The dusty fly on my windowsill.

You are my life flashing before my eyes.
The oil fire on the stove.
The nose hair I plucked in the mirror.
The stranger in the elevator
who stared at his shoes.

You are the plumber who charged me
110 bucks for five minutes work.

I remember your phone call.
I remember your knock on my door.

Dear Death: we race down the road,
toss empties at stop signs, wind whipping
our hair, your bony rattling on my dashboard.
You scream at bears like old friends.

Dear Death: you are my mother in the morning:
"Honey. Time to wake up."

You are the head nurse who told me
he'd never met someone more scared of dying.

Dear Death: you knock me off my feet.
You are the cop in the roadblock.
The muscle-head on the beach
a plague of baby oil slathered on his chest.
You are the mould that grows in our shower.

Dear Death: do you remember dancing
in the parking lot in your summer dress?
A symphony of carts crashing beside us.

I'm not done with you yet.
The water is boiled. The tea is on.
I remember you since the day I was born.
You're what keeps me loving this sliver of life.
You draw my squinting eyes to the sky.

Dear Death: you are just a dream.
Tell me what you know.
What you've been hiding all this time.

Notes

"A Good Window" is comprised of lines from Dale Carnegie's *Public Speaking and Influencing Men in Business* (1938).

"Nothing Between Us That Is Not Love" is from a line of Damian Rogers' "You Cannot Shed the Difficult, Most Stubborn Aspects of Your Nature with One Dose" (*Dear Leader*, 2015).

"Bargain of the Year" is comprised of text from *Popular Science, 1956.*

"After Reading a Bedtime Story to My Son" was written after Margaret Wise Brown's Goodnight Moon.

"When You Fall in Love with Your Babysitter" is for Cheryl MacKinnon, Miss Vancouver, 1974.

"The Long, Strange Trip" was based on dialogue from the documentary, *The Other One: The Long, Strange Trip of Bob Weir.*

"A Small Planet. A Big Wave" was written following the Indian Ocean Earthquake, December 26, 2004, that created tsunami waves that killed thousands in south Asia.

"No Shame in a Navel" was based on *"I Dream of Jeannie"* and NBC's "No Navel Edict", *where* Barbara Eden was forbidden to show her belly button.

"Durbar Square Disappears" was written following the April 25, 2015 Nepal earthquake that destroyed much of the Katmandu UNESCO World Heritage Site.

Acknowledgements

"There's Been a Terrible Mistake" was first published in *This Magazine* (July/August, 2006).

"No Shame in a Navel" appeared in *Maisonneuve* (online) for the Castaway Writing Contest Winner (August, 2007).

"Sleeping with bill" appeared in *radiant danse uv being, a poetic portrait of bill bissett* (Nightwood Editions, 2006).

"the day bill bissett blew into town" appeared in the following: *The Georgia Straight* (July, 2006); BC's *Poetry in Transit* (2006), a collection of poetry car cards and transit shelter ads, which feature the work of BC-authored and Canadian-published poets; and, *radiant danse uv being, a poetic portrait of bill bissett* (Nightwood Editions, 2006).

"One Dies One's Life" appeared in *Tattoos on Cedar: Volume Two*, Washington Poets Association Anthology (Reischling Press, 2006).

Plenty of thanks to... rox (aka Stephen Roxborough), editor extraordinaire, artist, mentor and friend, who for 36 years I've questioned, "Why sweep leaves from Granville Street?" bill bissett and his radiant danse uv being: "we dont no as much as r pomes." Stuart Ross, who kept asking, "How's the writing?" even when there was none. The Cobras, my childhood band of brothers. The madcapians of Chapman Camp. The Sakura Sushi chef who, as I write this, keeps passing me complimentary spicy salmon rolls. Dale Winslow, and her creative spirit in NeoPoiesis Press. My family who reminds me: love is round. My writing students, proof there is no beginning, and no end.

To death, our kick-ass reminder: we're still alive.

Jeff Pew is a high school counsellor and creative writing
teacher. He is co-editor, and Pushcart Prize nominee,
for *radiant danse uv being: a poetic portrait of bill bissett*
(Nightwood Editions, 2006). His poetry and journalism
have appeared in various magazines, BC's Poetry in
Transit, and on CBC radio. Jeff lives in Kimberley, BC
with Alison. They have two sons, Kalum and Noah.
One Foot In is his first collection of poetry.

NeoPoiesis: *a new way of making*

1) in ancient Greece, poiesis referred to the process of making: creation - production - organization - formation - causation

2) a process that can be physical and spiritual, biological and intellectual, artistic and technological, material and teleological, efficient and formal

3) a means of modifying the environment and a method of organizing the self, the making of art and music and poetry, the fashioning of memory and history and philosophy, the construction of perception and expression and reality

4) an independent publisher with a steadfast goal to print and promote outstanding poets, writers and artists that reflect the creative drive and spirit of the new electronic landscape

NeoPoiesisPress.com

www.ingramcontent.com/pod-product-compliance
Lightning Source LLC
Chambersburg PA
CBHW071353090426
42738CB00012B/3101